OPEN COURT READING

T**eacher's Annotated Editi**on

A Division of *The McGraw-Hill Companies*

Columbus, Ohio

D1402526

www.sra4kids.com

SRA/McGraw-Hill

A Division of The McGraw·Hill Companies

Send all inquiries to:
SRA/McGraw-Hill
8787 Orion Place
Columbus, OH 43240-4027

Printed in the United States of America.

ISBN 0-07-572049-3

2 3 4 5 6 7 8 9 QPD 07 06 05 04 03 02

Table of Contents

Unit 1 School

Lesson 1 *Unit Introduction*
Grammar, Usage, and Mechanics:
Words That Name People and Animals 2

Lesson 6 *Boomer Goes to School*
Grammar, Usage, and Mechanics:
Words That Name Objects 3

Lesson 11 *I Brought a Worm*
Grammar, Usage, and Mechanics:
Words That Name Places 4

Lesson 13 *Fine Art*
Letter Recognition: Recognizing a–g 5

Lesson 14 *Fine Art*
Letter Recognition: Writing a–h 6

Lesson 16 *Annabelle Swift, Kindergartner*
Letter Recognition:
Matching Capital and Small Letters 7

Lesson 16 *Annabelle Swift, Kindergartner*
Grammar, Usage, and Mechanics: Review 8

Lesson 19 *Annabelle Swift, Kindergartner*
Letter Recognition:
Matching Capital and Small Letters 9

Lesson 19 *Annabelle Swift, Kindergartner*
Writer's Craft: Letters to Words 10

Lesson 20 *Unit Wrap-Up*
Alphabetical Order: A–L 11

Unit 2 Shadows

Lesson 1 *Unit Introduction*
Grammar, Usage, and Mechanics: Sentence Types . . 12

Lesson 1 *Unit Introduction*
Writer's Craft: Words to Sentences 13

Lesson 2 *Shadows*
Letter Formation: Recognizing Ll–Nn 14

Lesson 3 *Shadows*
Alphabetical Order: A–R 15

Lesson 6 *Bear Shadow*
Grammar, Usage, and Mechanics: Capital Letters . . . 16

Lesson 9 *Bear Shadow*
Exploring Sounds and Letters:
Matching Capital and Small Letters 17

Lesson 11 *The Wolf and His Shadow*
Grammar, Usage, and Mechanics: End Marks 18

Lesson 12 *The Wolf and His Shadow*
Exploring Sounds and Letters:
Matching Capital and Small Letters 19

Lesson 14 *Fine Art*
Exploring Sounds and Letters:
Matching Capital and Small Letters 20

Lesson 14 *Fine Art*
Writer's Craft: Telling in Time Order 21

Lesson 16 *Nothing Sticks Like a Shadow*
Grammar, Usage, and Mechanics: Review 22

Lesson 17 *Nothing Sticks Like a Shadow*
Alphabetical Order: A–Z 23

Unit 3 Finding Friends

Lesson 1 *Unit Introduction*
Grammar, Usage, and Mechanics:
Words That Describe Color 24

Lesson 1 *Unit Introduction*
Writer's Craft: Collecting and Organizing Data 25

Lesson 4 *Ginger*
Phonics Skills: Identifying Initial Sounds 26

Lesson 6 *The Lonely Prince*
Grammar, Usage, and Mechanics:
Words That Describe How Many 27

Lesson 6 *The Lonely Prince*
Writer's Craft: Messages 28

Lesson 9 *The Lonely Prince*
Phonics Skills: Identifying Words 29

Lesson 11 *Making Friends*
Grammar, Usage, and Mechanics:
Words That Describe Weather 30

Lesson 14 *Fine Art*
Phonics Skills: Identifying Ending Sounds 31

Lesson 16 *Don't Need Friends*
Grammar, Usage, and Mechanics: Review 32

Lesson 19 *Don't Need Friends*
Phonics Skills: Identifying Short Vowel Sounds 33

Unit 4   The Wind

Lesson 1   *Unit Introduction*
Exploring Sounds and Letters: Initial Sound of S 34

Lesson 1   *Unit Introduction*
Grammar, Usage, and Mechanics:
Words That Describe Senses 35

Lesson 3   *Gilberto and the Wind*
Exploring Sounds and Letters: Ending Sound of S . . . 36

Lesson 4   *Gilberto and the Wind*
Exploring Sounds and Letters: Initial Sound of M . . . 37

Lesson 5   *Gilberto and the Wind*
Exploring Sounds and Letters: Ending Sound of M . . 38

Lesson 6   *What Happens When Wind Blows?*
Exploring Sounds and Letters:
Initial Sounds of S and M 39

Lesson 6   *What Happens When Wind Blows?*
Grammar, Usage, and Mechanics:
Words that Describe Position 40

Lesson 7   *What Happens When Wind Blows?*
Exploring Sounds and Letters: Initial Sound of D 41

Lesson 8   *What Happens When Wind Blows?*
Exploring Sounds and Letters: Ending Sound of D . . . 42

Lesson 9   *What Happens When Wind Blows?*
Exploring Sounds and Letters:
Ending Sounds of S, M, D 43

Lesson 10   *What Happens When Wind Blows?*
Exploring Sounds and Letters: Initial Sound of P 44

Lesson 11   *The Wind*
Matching Sounds and Letters: Ending Sound of P . . . 45

Lesson 11   *The Wind*
Grammar, Usage, and Mechanics:
Words That Show Action 46

Lesson 12   *The Wind*
Matching Sounds and Letters: Sound of Short A 47

Lesson 13   *Fine Art*
Matching Sounds and Letters: Identifying Words 48

Lesson 14   *Fine Art*
Matching Sounds and Letters: Initial Sound of H 49

Lesson 15   *The Wind*
Matching Sounds and Letters: Initial Sound of T 50

Lesson 16   *Wind Says Good Night*
Matching Sounds and Letters: Ending Sound of T . . . 51

Lesson 16   *Wind Says Good Night*
Grammar, Usage, and Mechanics: Review 52

Lesson 17   *Wind Says Good Night*
Matching Sounds and Letters: Sound of Short O 53

Lesson 18   *Wind Says Good Night*
Matching Sounds and Letters: Identifying Words 54

Lesson 19   *Wind Says Good Night*
Matching Sounds and Letters: Initial Sound of N 55

Lesson 20   *Unit Wrap-Up*
Matching Sounds and Letters: Ending Sound of N . . . 56

Unit 5   Stick To It

Lesson 1   *Unit Introduction*
Grammar, Usage, and Mechanics:
Words That Show Action 57

Lesson 2   *The Great Big Enormous Turnip*
Sounds and Spellings: Initial Sound of S 58

Lesson 4   *The Great Big Enormous Turnip*
Sounds and Spellings: Final Sound of M 59

Lesson 4   *The Great Big Enormous Turnip*
Writer's Craft: Current Events and Newspapers 60

Lesson 5   *The Great Big Enormous Turnip*
Matching Sounds and Letters:
Initial Sound of Short A 61

Lesson 6   *Tillie and the Wall*
Matching Sounds and Letters: Sound of Short A 62

Lesson 6   *Tillie and the Wall*
Grammar, Usage, and Mechanics:
Words That Show Action 63

Lesson 8   *Tillie and the Wall*
Matching Sounds and Letters: Initial Sound of T 64

Lesson 9   *Tillie and the Wall*
Writer's Craft: Time and Order Words 65

Lesson 11   *To Catch a Fish*
Grammar, Usage, and Mechanics:
Words That Show Action 66

Lesson 12   *To Catch a Fish*
Sounds and Spellings: Initial Sound of H 67

Lesson 13   *Fine Art*
Sounds and Spellings: Ending Sound of P 68

Lesson 14   *Fine Art*
Writer's Craft: Sentence Elaboration 69

Lesson 16   *Wanda's Roses*
Sounds and Spellings: Sound of Short I 70

Lesson 16   *Wanda's Roses*
Grammar, Usage, and Mechanics: Review 71

Lesson 17   *Wanda's Roses*
Sounds and Spellings: Alphabetical Order 72

Lesson 18   *Wanda's Roses*
Sounds and Spellings: Ending Sound of L 73

Unit 6   Red, White, and Blue

Lesson 1   *Unit Introduction*
Sounds and Spellings: Initial Sound of N 74

Lesson 1   *Unit Introduction*
Grammar, Usage, and Mechanics: Capital Letters . . . 75

Lesson 2   *Patriotism*
Sounds and Spellings: Ending Sound of N 76

Lesson 4   *Patriotism*
Matching Sounds and Letters: Initial Sound of D 77

Lesson 6   *Hats Off for the Fourth of July*
Sounds and Spellings: Sound of Short O 78

Lesson 6   *Hats Off for the Fourth of July*
Grammar, Usage, and Mechanics: Sentence Types . . 79

Lesson 7   *Hats Off for the Fourth of July*
Matching Sounds and Letters: Initial Sound of B 80

Lesson 8   *Hats Off for the Fourth of July*
Matching Sounds and Letters: Ending Sound of B . . . 81

Lesson 9   *Hats Off for the Fourth of July*
Writer's Craft: Location Words 82

Lesson 10   *Hats Off for the Fourth of July*
Matching Sounds and Letters: Initial Sound of C 83

Lesson 11   *America the Beautiful*
Grammar, Usage, and Mechanics: End Marks 84

Lesson 12   *America the Beautiful*
Sounds and Spellings: Initial Sound of R 85

Lesson 13   *Fine Art*
Sounds and Spellings: Ending Sound of R 86

Lesson 14   *Fine Art*
Writer's Craft: Sensory Detail 87

Lesson 15   *America the Beautiful*
Matching Sounds and Letters: Sound of Short U 88

Lesson 16   *The American Wei*
Sounds and Spellings: Initial Sound of G 89

Lesson 16   *The American Wei*
Grammar, Usage, and Mechanics: Review 90

Lesson 17   *The American Wei*
Sounds and Spellings: Ending Sound of G 91

Lesson 19   *The American Wei*
Sounds and Spellings: Initial Sound of J 92

Lesson 19   *The American Wei*
Writer's Craft: Staying on Topic 93

Unit 7   Teamwork

Lesson 1   *Unit Introduction*
Matching Sounds and Letters: Initial Sound of F 94

Lesson 1   *Unit Introduction*
Grammar, Usage, and Mechanics: Pronouns: I, You . . 95

Lesson 2   *Team Time!*
Sounds and Spellings: Ending Sound of F 96

Lesson 4   *Team Time!*
Matching Sounds and Letters: Sound of Short E 97

Lesson 5   *Team Time!*
Writer's Craft: End Rhyme 98

Lesson 6   *Swimmy*
Matching Sounds and Letters: Identifying Words 99

Lesson 6   *Swimmy*
Grammar, Usage, and Mechanics: Pronouns:
He, She, It 100

Lesson 7   *Swimmy*
Matching Sounds and Letters: Sound of Z 101

Lesson 8   *Swimmy*
Matching Sounds and Letters: Ending Sound of Z . . 102

Lesson 10   *Swimmy*
Matching Sounds and Letters: Initial Sound of W . . 103

Lesson 11   *Cleaning Up the Block*
Grammar, Usage, and Mechanics:
Pronouns: We, They 104

Lesson 12   *Cleaning Up the Block*
Sounds and Spellings: Initial Sound of K 105

Lesson 13   *Fine Art*
Matching Sounds and Letters: Ending Sound of K . . 106

Lesson 15   *Cleaning Up the Block*
Sounds and Spellings: Initial Sound of Q 107

Lesson 16   *The Little Red Hen*
Grammar, Usage, and Mechanics: Review 108

Lesson 17   *The Little Red Hen*
Matching Sounds and Letters: Initial Sound of Y . . . 109

Lesson 19   *The Little Red Hen*
Matching Sounds and Letters: Sound of V 110

Unit 8   By the Sea

Lesson 1   *Unit Introduction*
Phonics Skills: Identifying Words 111

Lesson 1   *Unit Introduction*
Grammar, Usage, and Mechanics: Review 112

Lesson 4   *The Ocean*
Phonics Skills: Identifying Words 113

Lesson 4   *The Ocean*
Writer's Craft: Asking and Answering Questions 114

Lesson 6   *Humphrey the Lost Whale*
Grammar, Usage, and Mechanics: Review 115

Lesson 7   *Humphrey the Lost Whale*
Phonics Skills: Identifying Words 116

Lesson 9   *Humphrey the Lost Whale*
Phonics Skills: Identifying Words 117

Lesson 11   *There Once Was a Puffin*
Grammar, Usage, and Mechanics: Review 118

Lesson 12   *There Once Was a Puffin*
Phonics Skills: Identifying Words 119

Lesson 14   *Fine Art*
Phonics Skills: Identifying Words 120

Lesson 14   *Fine Art*
Writer's Craft: Captions 121

Lesson 16   *Hello Ocean*
Grammar, Usage, and Mechanics: Review 122

Lesson 17   *Hello Ocean*
Phonics Skills: Identifying Words 123

Lesson 19   *Hello Ocean*
Writer's Craft: What Might Have Happened 124

Name _____ Date _____

▶ Words That Name: People and Animals

Directions: Listen as I read each word that names a person or an animal. Look at the pictures. Draw a line from the word to the picture it matches.

1. girl

2. bug

3. fox

4. man

▶ Words That Name: Objects

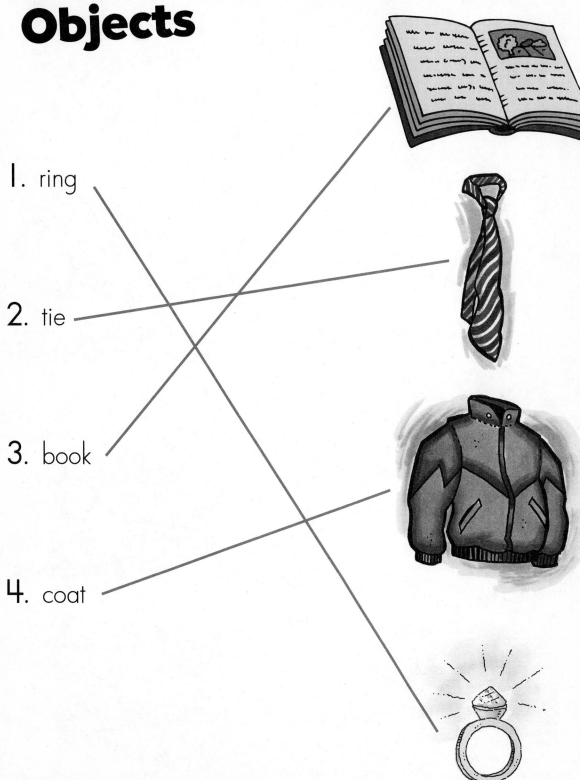

1. ring

2. tie

3. book

4. coat

GRAMMAR AND USAGE

Name _____ Date _____

▶ # Words That Name: Places

GRAMMAR AND USAGE

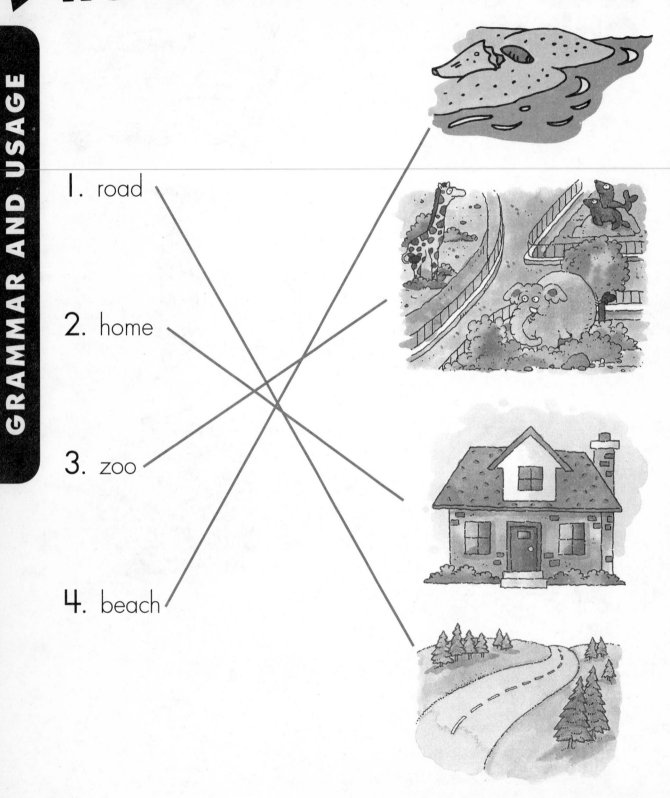

1. road

2. home

3. zoo

4. beach

Words That Name: Places • Challenge

▶Letter Recognition

Directions: Find and circle the small letters *a, b, c, d, e, f,* and *g.*

SOUNDS AND LETTERS

►Letter Recognition

Directions: Write the small letter for each capital letter.

SOUNDS AND LETTERS

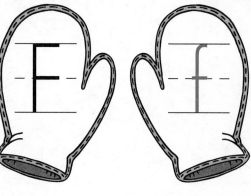

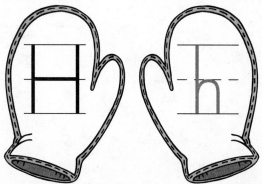

A   a   E   e

B   b   F   f

C   c   G   g

D   d   H   h

▶Letter Recognition

K   h   (k)   f   b

H   d   j   (h)   f

Directions: Circle the small letter that matches the capital letter. Then, color the flower petals that match the letter in the center of each flower.

SOUNDS AND LETTERS

UNIT 1 School • **Lesson 16** *Annabelle Swift, Kindergartner*

▶Review

Directions: Listen as I read each word that names a person, an animal, an object, or a place. Look at the pictures. Draw a line from the word to the picture it matches.

1. queen

2. zoo

3. fork

4. duck

Review • Challenge

UNIT 1 School • **Lesson 19** *Annabelle Swift, Kindergartner*

▶ Letter Recognition

Directions: Match the animals to their homes and the capital letters to their small letters.

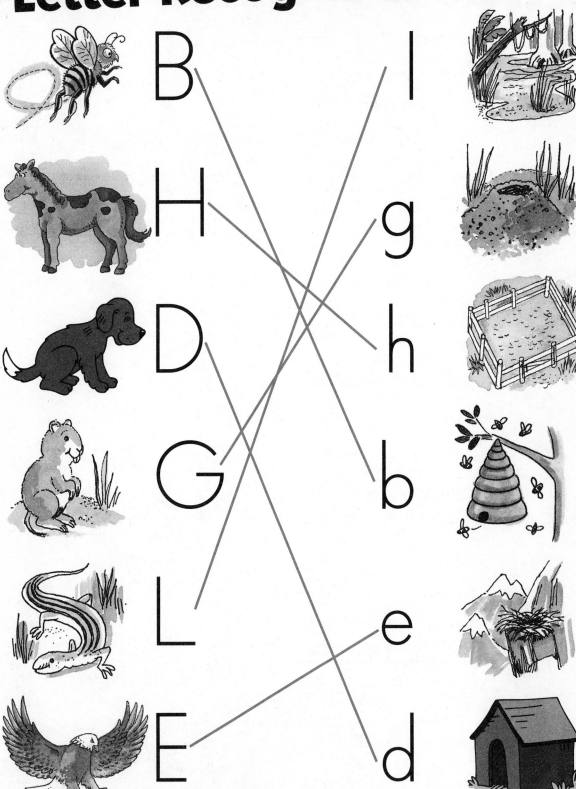

SOUNDS AND LETTERS

▶Letters to Words

Directions: Use the letters to spell a word.

WRITER'S CRAFT

1. o g

2. e m

3. o t

4. o y u

5. t i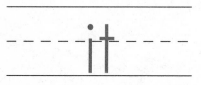

▶ **Alphabetical Order**

Directions: Draw a line connecting the capital letters in order from *A* to *L* to help the dog find its way home.

	A	B	C	D	E	F
A		K				G
C		K				H
L		K				I
F	C	J		L	K	J
M		N				D
E		O				L
B		P				B
K	G	C	D	I	F	H

SOUNDS AND LETTERS

▶Sentence Types: Statements and Questions

Directions: Listen as I read each sentence. Circle the sentence type I read.

[Teacher Direction: Statement]

1. (I read the blue book.) Where is your book?

[Teacher Direction: Question]

2. I am six years old. (How old are you?)

[Teacher Direction: Question]

3. (When is lunch?) We eat at noon.

[Teacher Direction: Statement]

4. Do you have a pet? (I have a turtle.)

UNIT 2 Shadows • **Lesson 1** *What Makes a Shadow?/Shadows*

▶ Words to Sentences

Directions: Listen as I read each sentence and the answers. Circle the missing word that completes the sentence.

1. I like to read _____. (books) bananas

2. I have a pet _____. sink (dog)

3. Ice is _____. soft (cold)

4. The sun is _____. (hot) blue

FORMING LETTERS

UNIT 2 Shadows • **Lesson 2** *Shadows*

▶ **Letter Formation**

Directions: Circle the capital and small forms of the letters *Ll, Mm,* and *Nn.*

SOUNDS AND LETTERS

C d H I

 A c D e

E a  F

f h A  G B

 b K  i j

I K J I  A

Letter Formation • Challenge

▶Alphabetical Order

Directions: Connect the dots in order from *A* to *R* to complete the picture of the sailboat.

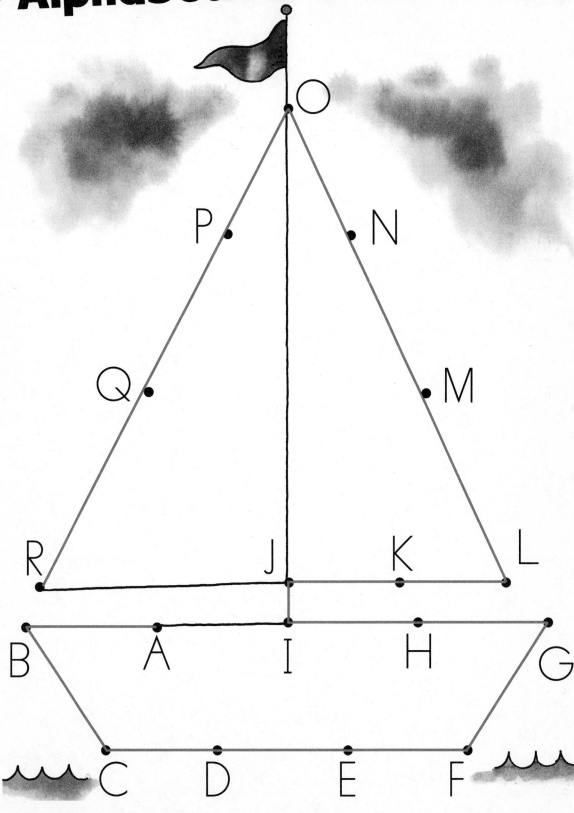

SOUNDS AND LETTERS

Name ____________________ Date __________

Capital Letters

MECHANICS

Directions: Listen as I read the words. Look at the words carefully. Circle the word that uses a capital letter.

1. Paul paul
2. i I
3. margo Margo
4. we We
5. The the
6. you You

UNIT 2 Shadows • **Lesson 9** *Bear Shadow*

▶Sounds and Letters

Directions: Draw a line between each capital letter and its matching small letter.

▶ End Marks

Directions: Listen as I read each sentence. Circle the correct end mark.

MECHANICS

1. Where are you   .   (?)

2. Red is my favorite color   (.)   ?

3. Her shoes were dirty   (.)   ?

4. Are you my teacher   .   (?)

Name _____ Date _____

▶ Sounds and Letters

Directions: Color the boxes that have the same three letters in each square.

T	t	T
h	L	K
F	R	j

E	R	V
d	r	n
a	R	a

v	D	R
u	V	A
n	I	v

q	b	p
Q	g	d
q	G	C

M	h	N
I	N	m
n	H	i

SOUNDS AND LETTERS

UNIT 2 Shadows • **Lesson 14** *Fine Art*

▶ Sounds and Letters

Directions: Draw a line from each capital letter to its matching small letter.

Sounds and Letters • **Challenge**

UNIT 2 Shadows • **Lesson 14** *The Wolf and His Shadow*

▶Telling in Time Order

First, I woke up. Next, I ate breakfast.

Drawings will vary, but they should make sense with the text.

WRITER'S CRAFT

▶**Review**

Directions: Listen as I read each sentence. Circle the correct sentence.

1. the horse jumped   (The horse jumped.)

2. (Where is the phone?)   where is the Phone

3. did you practice   (Did you practice?)

4. (The room is small.)   the room is small?

▶ Alphabetical Order

Directions: Draw a line connecting the small letters in order from a to z.

SOUNDS AND LETTERS

Name _____ Date _____

▶ Words That Describe: Color

GRAMMAR AND USAGE

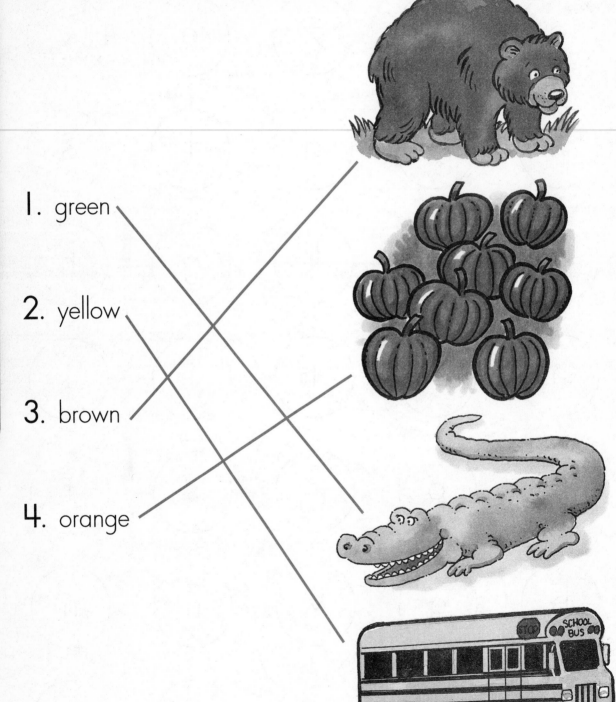

1. green

2. yellow

3. brown

4. orange

Words That Describe: Color • Challenge

▶Organizing and Collecting Data

Directions: Listen as I read the list of words that name animals. Put an X over the words that do not name an animal.

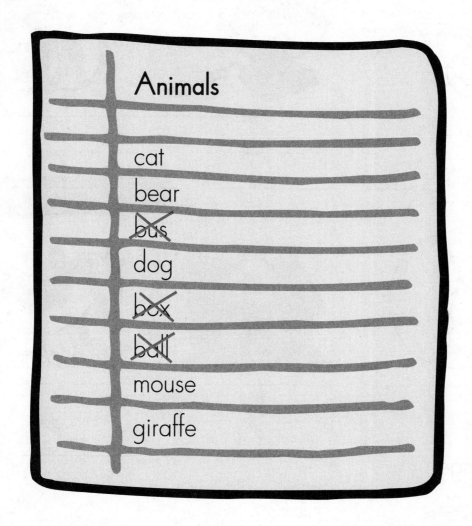

Animals

cat
bear
~~bus~~
dog
~~box~~
~~ball~~
mouse
giraffe

UNIT 3 Finding Friends • **Lesson 4** *Ginger*

▶Phonics Skills

Directions: Write the letter that each picture begins with.

SOUNDS AND LETTERS

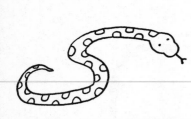

s

f

m

b

h

d

p

r

t

Phonics Skills • **Challenge**

▶ Words That Describe: How Many

Directions: Listen to the words that describe how many that I read and look at the number. Draw a line from the number to the picture it matches.

two   2

one   1

five   5

three   3

UNIT 3 Finding Friends • **Lesson 6** *The Lonely Prince*

▶Messages

WRITER'S CRAFT

1. (Mom, we went for a walk.)
   walk

2. (Your Uncle Max called.)
   phone

3. (Please wash the car.)
   water

4. (Great work!)
   paper

Messages • **Challenge**

UNIT 3 **Finding Friends • Lesson 9** *The Lonely Prince*

▶ Phonics Skills

fan	bibs	ham	bat	pins

Directions: Find the word that names each picture. Write each word on the line below the correct picture.

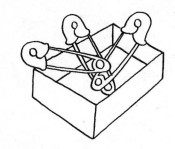

pins

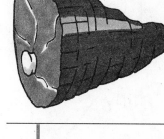

ham

bibs

bat

fan

Name _____ Date _____

▶ Words That Describe: Weather

GRAMMAR AND USAGE

1. rainy

2. sunny

3. snowy

Directions: Listen as I read each word that describes weather. Draw a line from the word to the picture it matches.

UNIT 3 **Finding Friends • Lesson 14** *Fine Art*

▶Phonics Skills

be d

ma n

ban d

mo p

po t

SOUNDS AND LETTERS

Name _____ Date _____

GRAMMAR AND USAGE

▶**Review**

Drawings will vary, but they should match the word that describes.

Directions: Listen as I read the words that describe. Draw a picture that matches each word.

I. purple

2. four

3. rainy

UNIT 3 Finding Friends • **Lesson 19** *Don't Need Friends*

▶ Phonics Skills

Directions: Draw a line to the letter that correctly completes each word.

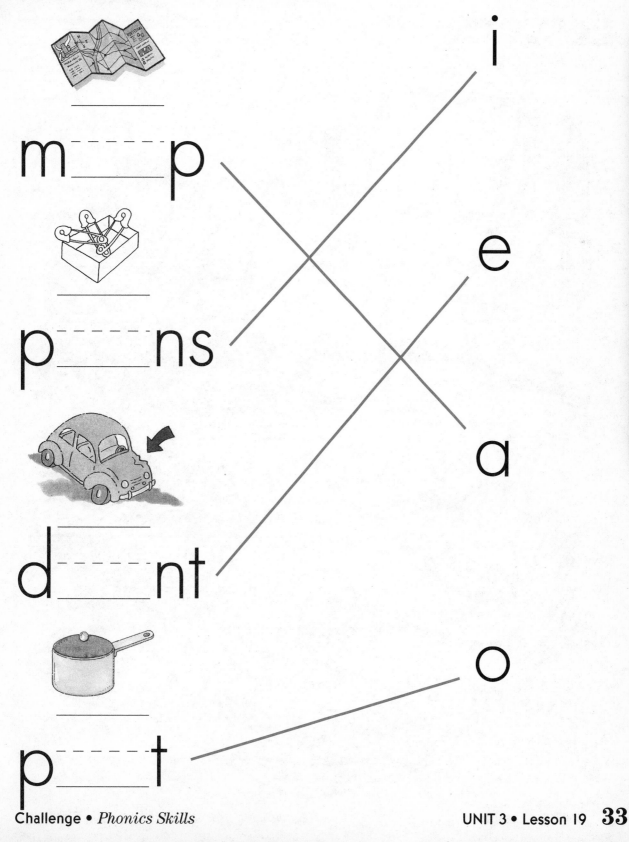

m___p

p___ns

d___nt

p___t

i

e

a

o

▶ Exploring Sounds and Letters

Directions: Circle each picture whose name begins with /s/.

▶ Words That Describe: Senses

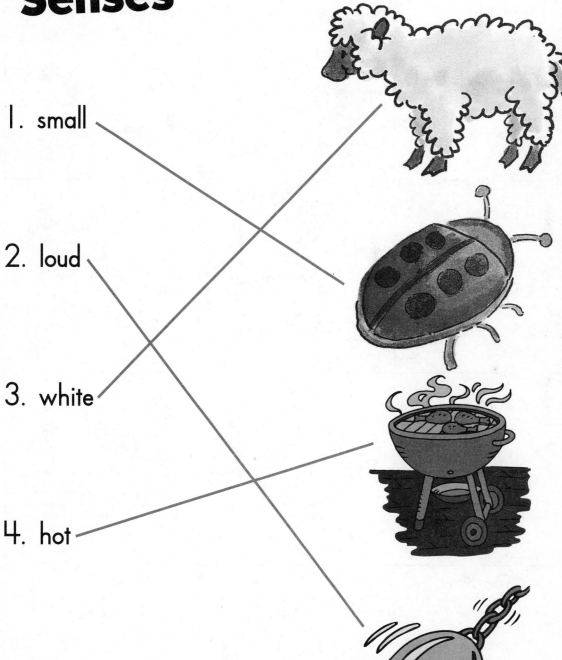

1. small

2. loud

3. white

4. hot

GRAMMAR AND USAGE

Name _____ Date _____

▶ Sounds and Letters

SOUNDS AND LETTERS

Directions: Color each picture whose name ends with /s/.

Sounds and Letters • Challenge

▶Sounds and Letters

Directions: Draw a line from the letters *Mm* to each picture whose name begins with /m/.

SOUNDS AND LETTERS

▶Sounds and Letters

Directions: Draw a line from the letters *Mm* to each picture whose name ends with /m/.

Sounds and Letters • Challenge

The Wind • Lesson 6 *What Happens When Wind Blows?*

▶ Sounds and Letters

Directions: Color red each picture whose name begins with /s/. Color blue each picture whose name begins with /m/.

SOUNDS AND LETTERS

Challenge • *Sounds and Letters*

UNIT 4 The Wind • **Lesson 6** *What Happens When Wind Blows?*

▶ Words That Describe: Position

GRAMMAR AND USAGE

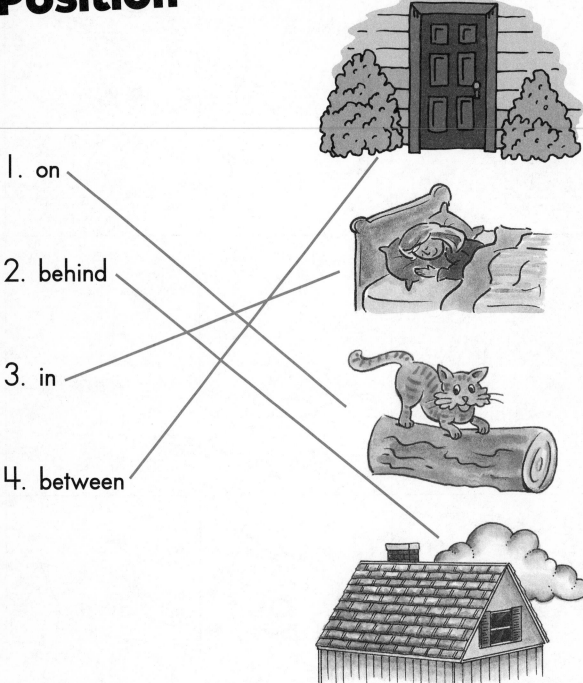

1. on

2. behind

3. in

4. between

Words That Describe: Position • Challenge

▶ Sounds and Letters

Directions: Draw a line from the letters *Dd* to each picture whose name begins with /d/.

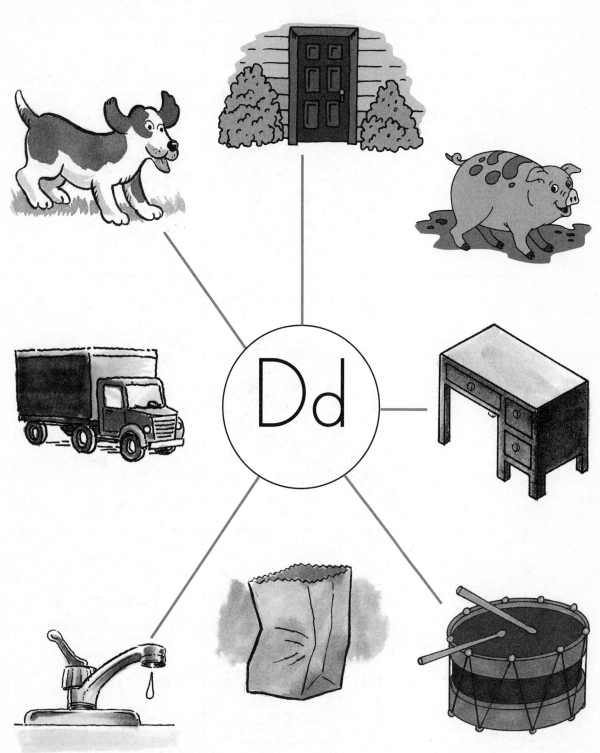

UNIT 4 The Wind • **Lesson 8** *What Happens When Wind Blows?*

►Sounds and Letters

Directions: Color each picture whose name ends with /d/.

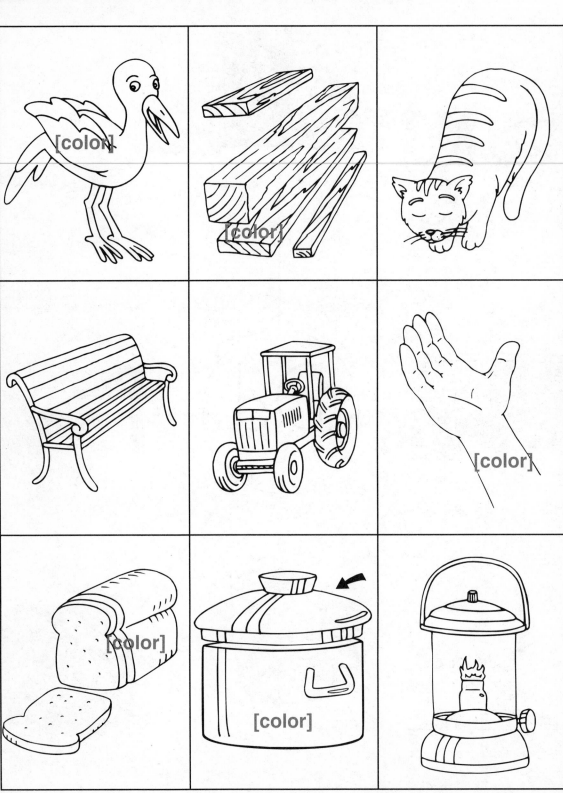

Sounds and Letters • **Challenge**

▶Sounds and Letters

Directions: Draw a line connecting the pictures whose names end with the same sound.

___d

___s

___m

___d

___s

___m

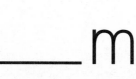

SOUNDS AND LETTERS

▶ Sounds and Letters

SOUNDS AND LETTERS

Directions: Circle each picture whose name begins with /p/.

▶ Matching Sounds and Letters

Directions: Draw a line connecting the letters *Pp* with each picture whose name ends with /p/.

SOUNDS AND LETTERS

▶ Words That Show Action

Directions: Listen as I read the words that show action. Draw a line from the word to the picture of the action.

GRAMMAR AND USAGE

1. hug

2. sleep

3. jump

4. hang

Words That Show Action • Challenge

▶ Matching Sounds and Letters

Directions: Circle each thing in the picture whose name has short /a/.

▶ Matching Sounds and Letters

Directions: Find the word at the bottom of the page that names each picture. Write that word below the picture.

sad

pad

sap

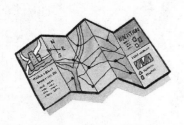

map

mad

| pad | mad | sap | map | sad |

Name _____ Date _____

▶Matching Sounds and Letters

Directions: Circle each thing in the picture whose name begins with /h/.

SOUNDS AND LETTERS

UNIT 4 The Wind • **Lesson 15** *The Wind*

► Matching Sounds and Letters

Directions: Color each picture whose name begins with /t/.

[color]		
[color]	[color]	
	[color]	[color]

Matching Sounds and Letters • Challenge

Name _____ Date _____

▶ Matching Sounds and Letters

Directions: Draw a line connecting the letters *Tt* with each picture whose name ends with /t/.

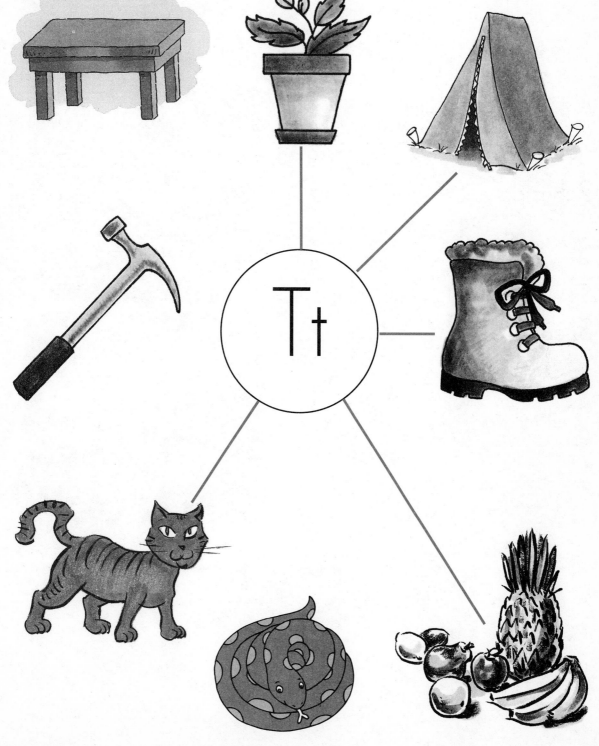

▶Review

GRAMMAR AND USAGE

1. soft

2. beside

3. eat

Directions: Listen to the words I read. Draw a line from the word to the picture it matches.

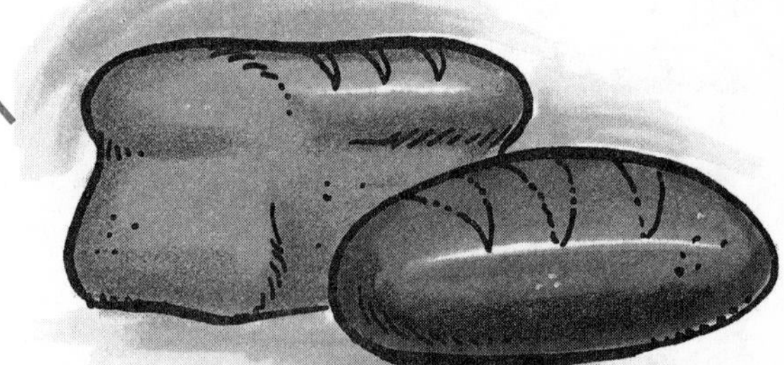

▶ Matching Sounds and Letters

Directions: Help the boy reach the bike shop by drawing a line connecting the pictures whose names have short /o/.

SOUNDS AND LETTERS

▶Matching Sounds and Letters

Directions: Find the word at the bottom of the page that names each picture. Write that word below the picture.

hot

top

mop

pot

dot

| dot   top   hot   mop   pot |

▶ Matching Sounds and Letters

Directions: Circle each thing in the picture whose name begins with /n/.

UNIT 4 **The Wind • Lesson 20** *Unit Wrap-Up*

▶ Matching Sounds and Letters

Directions: Circle each picture whose name ends with /n/.

[color]	[color]	
	[color]	[color]
	[color]	

Matching Sounds and Letters • Challenge

Name _____ Date _____

▶ Words That Show Action

Directions: Listen as I read each sentence. Underline the word that shows action.

1. We <u>walk</u> to the library.

2. He <u>reads</u> after dinner.

3. I <u>ride</u> my bike with my dad.

4. She <u>looks</u> for her coat.

5. They <u>jump</u> rope at recess.

6. We <u>listen</u> to the teacher.

GRAMMAR AND USAGE

▶ Sounds and Spelling

Directions: Color the sections that have s to reveal a hidden picture. Then, write the letter that goes with the initial sound of the picture.

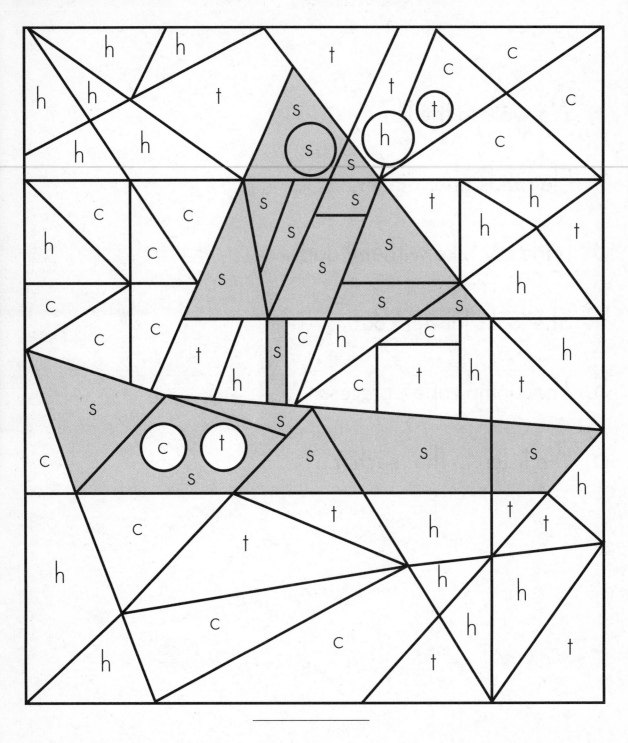

_____

_ _ _ _ _
S

UNIT 5 Stick to It • **Lesson 4** *The Great Big Enormous Turnip*

►Sounds and Spelling

Directions: Color the sections with the letter *Mm* to reveal the hidden picture. Then, write the letter that goes with the final sound of the picture.

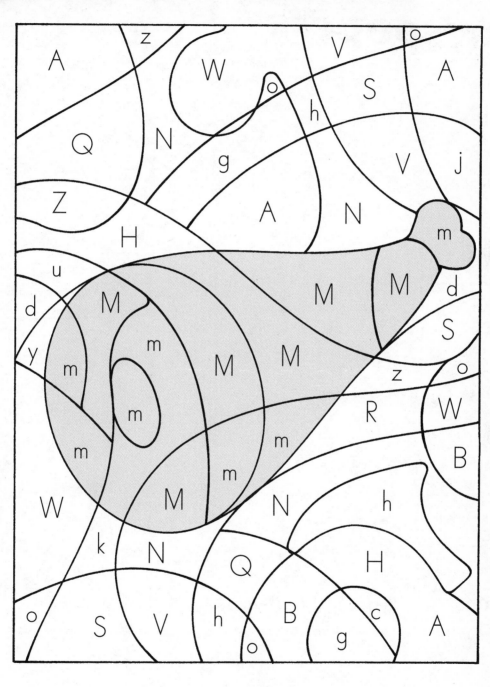

WRITER'S CRAFT

▶Current Events and Newspapers

Directions: Listen as I read the following list. Some things can be found in a newspaper, some things cannot. Put an X over the things that are not in a newspaper.

pictures

~~books~~

articles

names

~~apples~~

titles

stories

~~crayons~~

▶ Matching Sounds and Letters

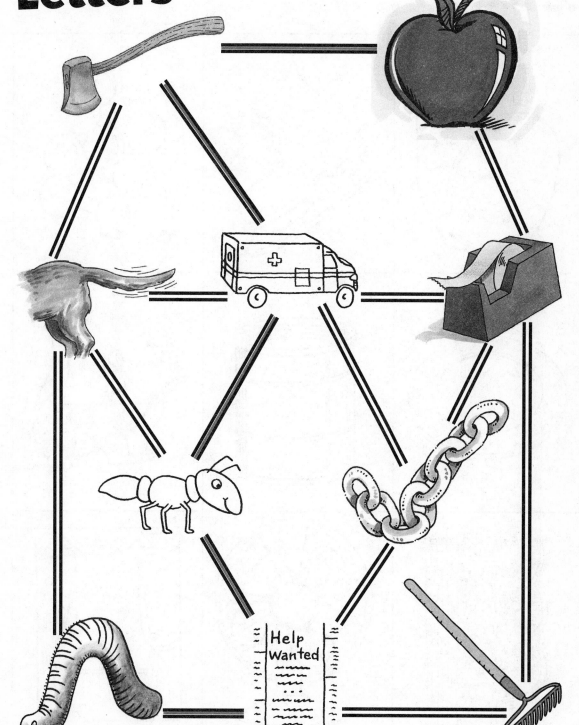

SOUNDS AND LETTERS

▶ Matching Sounds and Letters

Directions: Color each picture whose name has /a/.

[color]

[color]

[color]

[color]

[color]

▶ Words That Show Action: Tense, Present and Past

[Teacher Directions: Past]

1. I paint pictures. <u>He painted the fence.</u>

[Teacher Directions: Present]

2. She liked oranges. <u>I like oranges.</u>

[Teacher Directions: Present]

3. <u>The teacher smiles.</u> The principal smiled.

[Teacher Directions: Past]

4. They laugh. <u>We laughed.</u>

GRAMMAR AND USAGE

UNIT 5 **Stick to It • Lesson 8** *Tillie and the Wall*

▶ Sounds and Letters

Directions: Circle each picture whose name begins with /t/.

Sounds and Letters • Challenge

▶ Time and Order Words

1. (Today,) I read a book.

2. (Yesterday,) we rode bikes.

3. (Then,) it was time for a nap.

4. (Tomorrow,) I will go to school.

WRITER'S CRAFT

UNIT 5 Stick to It • **Lesson 11** *To Catch a Fish*

Directions: Listen as I read the sentences. Underline the sentence that uses the tense I read.

GRAMMAR AND USAGE

►Words That Show Action: Past, Present, and Future Tenses

[Teacher Directions: Future]

1. They ran. <u>We will run.</u>

[Teacher Directions: Past]

2. <u>She kicked the ball.</u> He kicks the ball.

[Teacher Directions: Present]

3. You will draw at home. <u>We draw in class.</u>

[Teacher Directions: Future]

4. <u>I will write you a letter.</u> You wrote me first.

UNIT 5   Stick to It • **Lesson 12** *To Catch a Fish*

▶ Sounds and Spelling

Directions: Color each picture whose name begins with /h/. Then draw the path through the pictures to help the girl get home.

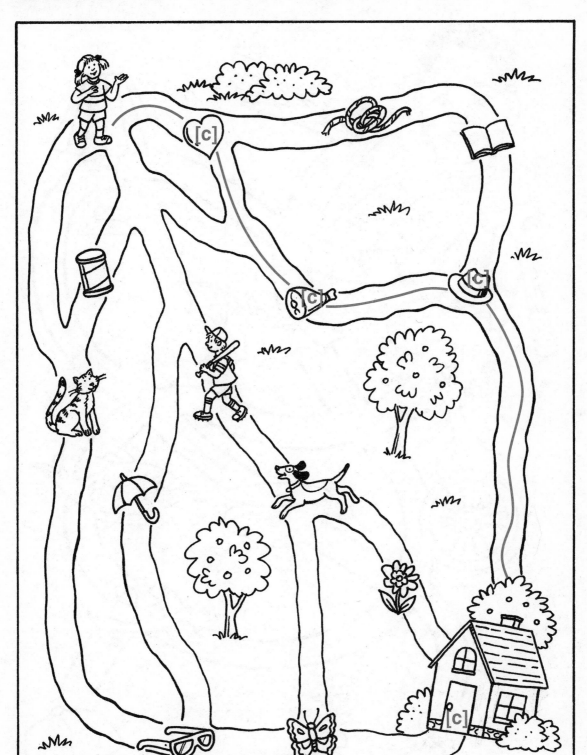

▶Sounds and Spelling

Directions: Color the pictures whose names end with /p/. Then, draw the path connecting the pictures to help the boy find his cap.

SOUNDS AND LETTERS

UNIT 5 **Stick to It • Lesson 14** *Fine Art*

▶Sentence Elaboration

1. I went swimming. (at the beach) again

2. He likes to draw. too (with crayons)

3. She plays soccer. also (at school)

4. We talked. (on the phone) soon

WRITER'S CRAFT

Name _____ Date _____

▶ Sounds and Spelling

SOUNDS AND LETTERS

▶Review

Directions: Listen as I read the sentences. Underline only the word that shows action in the tense I read.

[Teacher Directions: Past]

1. We <u>talked</u> on the phone yesterday.

[Teacher Directions: Future]

2. I <u>will wear</u> my favorite shirt.

[Teacher Directions: Present]

3. I <u>eat</u> vegetable soup.

[Teacher Directions: Future]

4. She <u>will throw</u> the ball to you.

GRAMMAR AND USAGE

▶ Sounds and Spelling

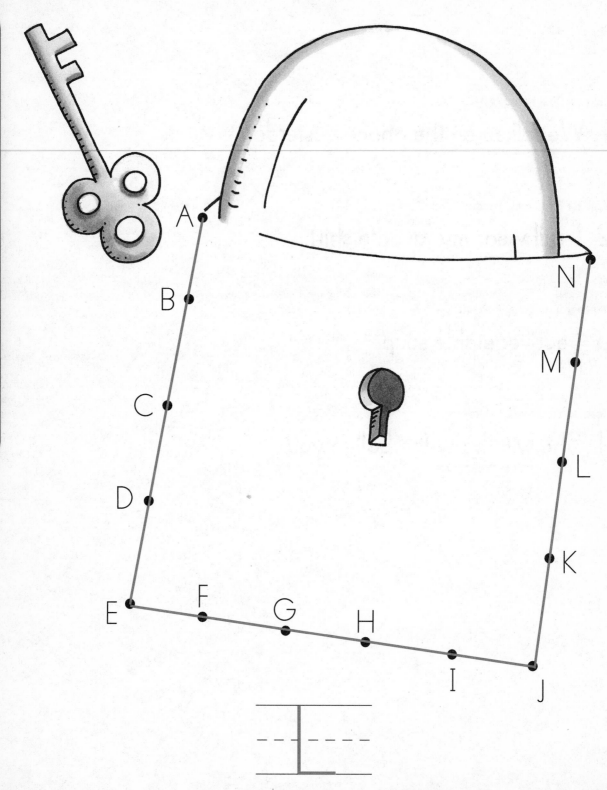

Directions: Connect the letters in order and then color the picture. Write the first letter of the name of the picture on the line.

Sounds and Spelling • Challenge

▶Sounds and Spelling

Directions: Color the pictures whose names end with /l/.

▶ Sounds and Spelling

Directions: Help the bird find its nest by following the path of pictures whose name begins with /ŋ/.

SOUNDS AND LETTERS

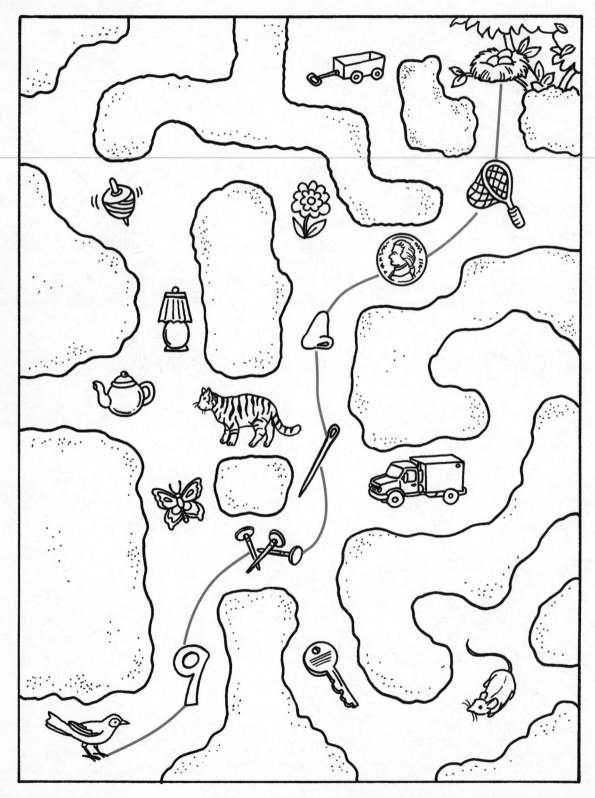

Sounds and Spellings • **Challenge**

▶ Capital Letters

1. 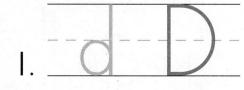 do you know William?

2. 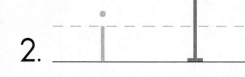 She and i went to the store.

3.  How old is Aunt carol?

4.  elephants are gray.

MECHANICS

▶Sounds and Spelling

Directions: Color all the items in the picture that end with /n/.

Sounds and Spelling • Challenge

UNIT 6 Red, White, and Blue • **Lesson 4** *Patriotism*

▶Sounds and Letters

Directions: Color each picture whose name begins with /d/.

SOUNDS AND LETTERS

▶ Sounds and Spelling

Directions: Circle each picture whose name has /o/.

SOUNDS AND LETTERS

Sounds and Spelling • Challenge

▶ Sentence Types

Directions: Listen as I read the sentences and the sentence type. Circle the missing end mark to match the sentence type.

[Teacher: Exclamation]

1. That's great   .   ?   (**!**)

[Teacher: Question]

2. Where do you live   .   (**?**)   !

[Teacher: Statement]

3. I live in Georgia   (**.**)   ?   !

[Teacher: Exclamation]

4. You're the best   .   ?   (**!**)

GRAMMAR AND USAGE

UNIT 6 Red, White, and Blue • **Lesson 7** *Hats Off for the Fourth of July!*

▶ Sounds and Letters

Directions: Draw a line connecting the letters *Bb* with each picture whose name begins with /b/.

Sounds and Letters • Challenge

▶ Sounds and Letters

Directions: Begin at the arrow and take the most direct route to the star by drawing a line that connects the pictures whose names end with /b/.

SOUNDS AND LETTERS

▶ Location Words

Directions: Listen as I read each sentence. Circle the location word.

WRITER'S CRAFT

1. The cow is (behind) the barn.

2. The bird is (above) the tree.

3. The garage is (between) the road and the house.

4. The book is (on) the shelf.

5. The cat is (under) the bed.

6. The bread is (in) the oven.

UNIT 6 Red, White, and Blue • **Lesson 10** *Hats Off for the Fourth of July!*

▶ Sounds and Letters

Directions: Circle each picture whose name begins with /k/.

Challenge • Sounds and Letters

UNIT 6 • Lesson 10 **83**

UNIT 6 Red, White, and Blue • **Lesson II** *America the Beautiful*

▶ End Marks

Directions: Listen as I read the sentences and the sentence type. Look at the end marks at the top of the page. Write the missing end mark to match the sentence type.

.	?	!

MECHANICS

[Teacher: Statement]

1. I enjoy reading ___

[Teacher: Question]

2. What do you read ___

[Teacher: Exclamation]

3. I love books ___

End Marks • Challenge

UNIT 6 Red, White, and Blue • **Lesson 12** *America the Beautiful*

▶Sounds and Spelling

SOUNDS AND LETTERS

▶ Sounds and Spelling

SOUNDS AND LETTERS

Directions: Draw a picture of something whose name ends with /r/. Then, write the letter r under the picture.

_____

_ _ _ _ r

Sounds and Spelling • **Challenge**

▶ Sensory Detail

Directions: Listen as I read each sentence. Circle the word that shows sensory detail.

1. The plate is too (warm) to hold.

2. The library is a (quiet) place.

3. My dog has (soft) fur.

4. The lemons are (sour.)

5. Is that your (white) shirt?

6. The brick is (heavy.)

WRITER'S CRAFT

▶ Sounds and Letters

Directions: Help the frog hop to the pond. Circle only those rocks with pictures whose names have /u/.

Sounds and Letters • Challenge

▶Sounds and Spelling

Directions: Draw a gift that begins with /g/ inside the gift box.

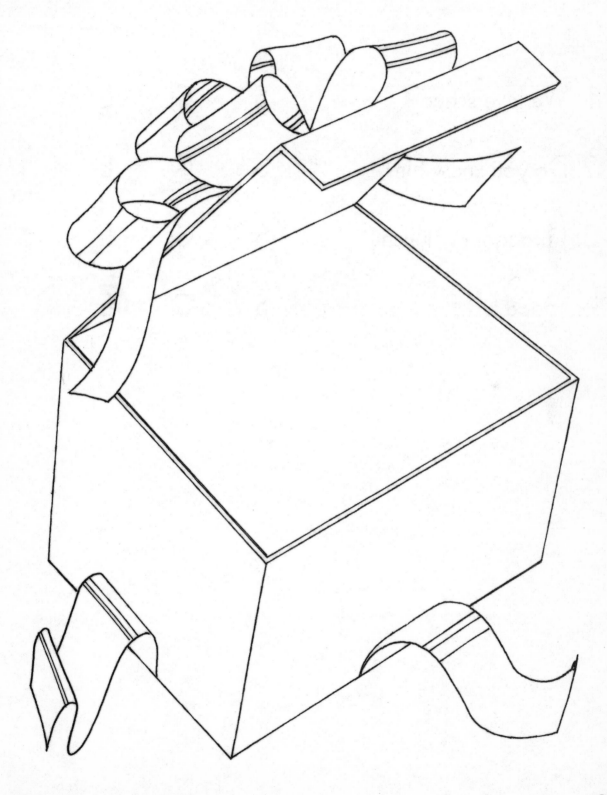

SOUNDS AND LETTERS

Name _____ Date _____

▶Review

GRAMMAR AND USAGE

Directions: Listen as I read each sentence. Underline the capital letters. Circle the end mark and the sentence type: S for statement, Q for question, and E for exclamation.

1. <u>W</u>e love school!   S   Q   **(E)**

2. <u>D</u>o you know him?   S   **(Q)**   E

3. <u>I</u> brought my lunch.   **(S)**   Q   E

4. <u>G</u>ood luck!   S   Q   **(E)**

▶Sounds and Spelling

Gg

Directions: Draw a line from *Gg* to the pictures whose names end with /g/. Then, write the words on the line.

dog   pig   log

UNIT 6 Red, White, and Blue • **Lesson 19** *The American Wei*

▶Sounds and Spelling

j

Sounds and Spelling • Challenge

▶Staying on Topic

1. The duck likes water. ~~I am six years old.~~ The duck is swimming.

2. It is raining today. Do you have an umbrella? ~~I like apples.~~

3. ~~My house is white and green.~~ We went to the library. The library has my favorite books.

4. He plays the piano. ~~She has a pet fish.~~ He practices the piano after school.

▶ **Sounds and Letters**

SOUNDS AND LETTERS

Directions: Draw a line connecting the letters *Ff* with each picture whose name begins with /f/.

Ff

Sounds and Letters • **Challenge**

UNIT 7 Teamwork • **Lesson 1** *Mr. McGill Goes to Town*

▶ Pronouns: I and You

Directions: Listen as I read each sentence without the pronoun. Circle the pronoun *I* or *you* to complete the sentence.

1. [I / You] am sleeping.

2. [I / You] were at home.

3. [I / You] were jogging.

4. [I / You] am making lunch.

GRAMMAR AND USAGE

▶Sounds and Spelling

Directions: Color each picture whose name ends with /f/.

Sounds and Spelling • Challenge

▶Sounds and Letters

Directions: Draw a line connecting the picture in the center with each picture whose name has the same /e/ sound.

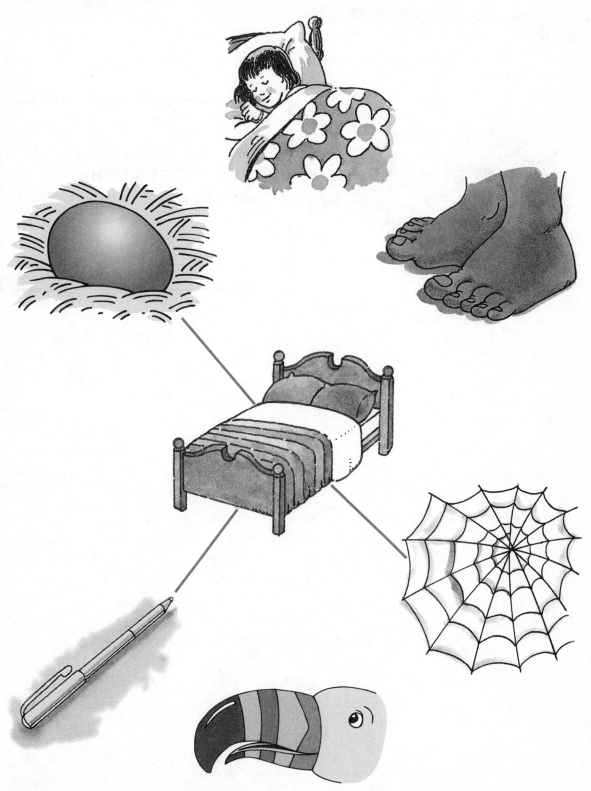

SOUNDS AND LETTERS

UNIT 7 Teamwork • **Lesson 5** *Teamwork*

▶Sound of Language: End Rhyme

Directions: Draw a picture in the second box of a word that rhymes with the picture in the first box.

WRITER'S CRAFT

cat

[Drawings will vary, but should rhyme with cat.]

▶Sounds and Letters

wax

box

fox

ax

mix

| ax | box | fox | wax | mix |

SOUNDS AND LETTERS

▶Pronouns: He, She, It

Directions: Look at the picture. Circle the pronoun *he, she,* or *it* that matches the picture.

GRAMMAR AND USAGE

1.  he   she   (it)

2.  he   (she)   it

3.  (he)   she   it

4.  he   she   (it)

Name _____ Date _____

▶ Sounds and Letters

Directions: Draw a picture of a zebra at the zoo and a buzzing bee.

▶ Sounds and Letters

Directions: Find the word at the bottom of the page that names each picture. Write that word below the picture.

SOUNDS AND LETTERS

flows

sneeze

squeeze

eyes

| eyes | squeeze | sneeze | flows |

UNIT 7 Teamwork • **Lesson 10** *Swimmy*

▶Sounds and Letters

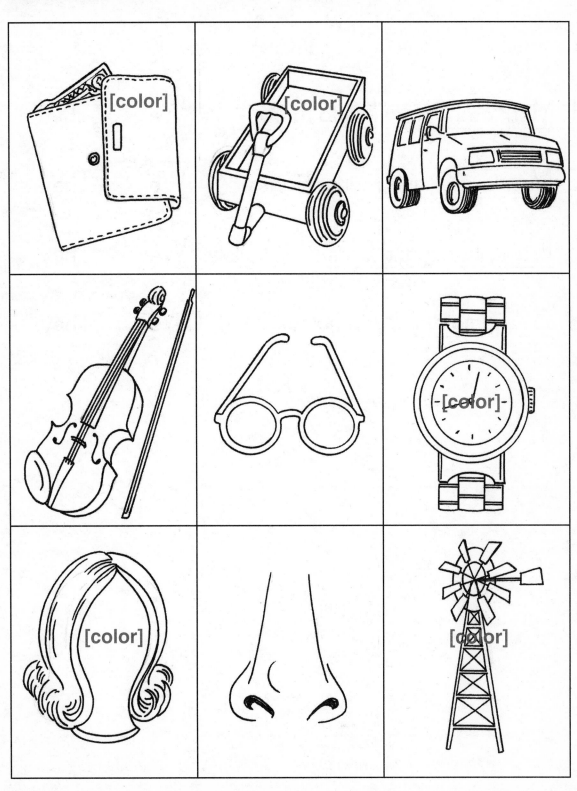

Challenge • *Sounds and Letters*

▶ Pronouns: We and They

GRAMMAR AND USAGE

1. <u>Mark and Sonya</u> like to run.   We   (They)

2. <u>Mrs. Carter and I</u> write stories.   (We)   They

3. <u>Frank, Irene, and Sam</u> play ball.   We   (They)

4. <u>Grandma and I</u> ride horses.   (We)   They

▶Sounds and Spelling

Directions: Circle something in the first picture that starts with /k/. Then, draw a picture of something that begins with /k/ in the treasure chest.

SOUNDS AND LETTERS

▶Sounds and Letters

Directions: Help the duck reach the lake by following the path that connects the pictures whose names end with /k/.

Sounds and Letters • **Challenge**

▶Sounds and Spelling

SOUNDS AND LETTERS

▶Review

Directions: Listen as I read the story and the pronoun box carefully. Circle any pronouns you hear or see in the story.

GRAMMAR AND USAGE

I	you	he	she	it	we	they

My class went on a field trip. (We) went to the zoo. Jeff and Calley sat behind me. (He) is her brother. (She) and Jeff are my friends. (I) saw an elephant. (It) was drinking water. Have (you) been to the zoo? (They) were helpful at the zoo.

▶Sounds and Letters

Directions: Draw a line connecting the letters *Yy* with each picture whose name begins with /y/.

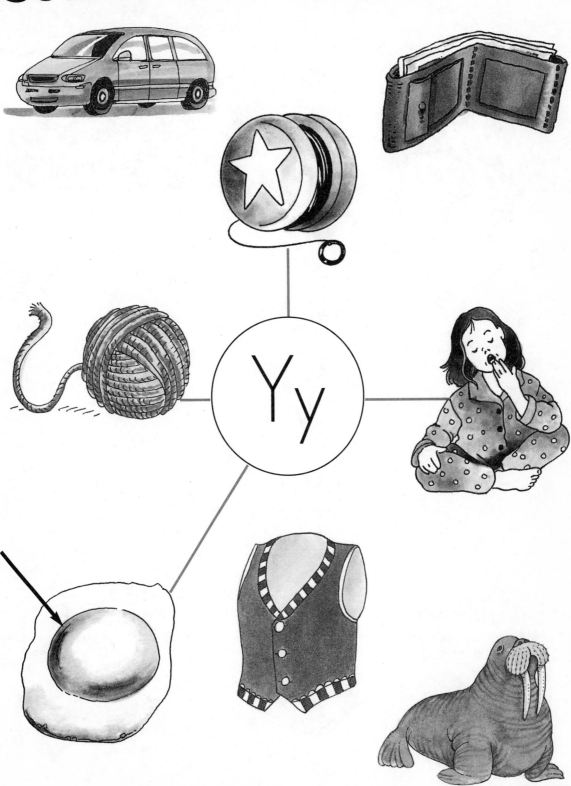

SOUNDS AND LETTERS

▶ Sounds and Letters

Directions: Draw a line connecting the letters Vv with each picture whose name begins or ends with /v/.

SOUNDS AND LETTERS

Sounds and Letters • **Challenge**

▶ Phonics Skills

The ___cat___ is sleeping.

You need to ___mix___ the batter.

Does the ___plant___ need water?

mix	plant	cat

SOUNDS AND LETTERS

UNIT 8 **By the Sea • Lesson I** *A Walk by the Seashore*

▶Review

GRAMMAR AND USAGE

Directions: Listen as I read each word that names. Draw a picture of the word that names in the box below it.

teacher

horse

hat

park

Drawings should match the word that names.

UNIT 8 By the Sea • **Lesson 4** *The Ocean*

▶Phonics Skills

The _clam_ lives in water.

Is the _truck_ still there?

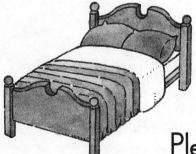

Please make your _bed_.

Directions: Find the word at the bottom of the page that completes each sentence. Write that word in the space provided.

truck	clam	bed

▶ # Asking and Answering Questions

1. What time is it?   My name is Tracie.

2. What is your name?   I am five years old.

3. How old are you?   I like elephants.

4. What is your favorite animal?   It is 2:30 p.m.

Name _____ Date _____

▶Review

Directions: Listen as I read the story. Circle any words that show action you hear or see.

We (swim) at the beach. We (build) sandcastles at the beach. We (play) volleyball at the beach. We (eat) lunch at the beach. We (walk) and (run) on the beach. And, we (sleep) on the beach.

GRAMMAR AND USAGE

▶Phonics Skills

Directions: Find the word at the bottom of the page that completes each sentence. Write that word in the space provided.

SOUNDS AND LETTERS

I stepped on a _____ twig _____.

Tom used a __ hammer __.

She found an _____ egg _____ in the nest.

hammer	egg	twig

UNIT 8 **By the Sea • Lesson 9** *Humphrey the Lost Whale*

▶ Phonics Skills

Steve's _____cuff_____ was white.

Did the sink _____drip_____ ?

The _____grass_____ needs to be cut.

grass	drip	cuff

SOUNDS AND LETTERS

▶Review

Directions: Listen as I read the words that describe. Draw a line from the word to the picture it describes.

1. yellow

2. five

3. sunny

4. soft

5. on

▶ **Phonics Skills**

SOUNDS AND LETTERS

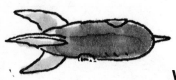

We saw the ___rocket___ take off.

Our new ___van___ was silver.

Did Ted lose his ___wallet___?

| wallet | rocket | van |

▶ Phonics Skills

Directions: Find the word at the bottom of the page that completes each sentence. Write that word in the space provided.

SOUNDS AND LETTERS

Let's ___ wax ___ the car.

Wendy dropped her ___ pen ___.

Was the ___ duck ___ in the water?

wax	duck	pen

Name _____ Date _____

▶ Captions

The ___park___ is empty.

WRITER'S CRAFT

▶**Review**

GRAMMAR, USAGE, AND MECHANICS

Directions: Listen as I read the story. Circle the capital letters and end marks you see. When you have finished, as a group, tell me the sentence type of what I read: statement, question, or exclamation.

[exclamation]   [statement]
I'm so excited! It's time for our family vacation.

[statement]   [statement]
Sometimes we go to Maine. This time we are going to

[exclamation]   [question]
South Carolina. I can't wait! Have you ever been there?

[statement]
We are going to have fun in South Carolina.

UNIT 8 By the Sea • **Lesson 17** *Hello Ocean*

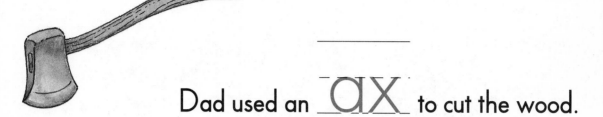

▶ Phonics Skills

SOUNDS AND LETTERS

Dad used an ___ax___ to cut the wood.

My ___zipper___ is stuck.

I like to wear my new ___watch___.

watch	zipper	ax

WRITER'S CRAFT

▶ What Might Have Happened

Directions: Look at the picture. Draw a picture of what might have happened *before* the picture.

Drawings will vary, but they should make sense with the picture.